ELLIOTT SOLAK

Facts About the Emu

By Lisa Strattin

© 2019 Lisa Strattin

D1608161

FREE BOOK

FREE FOR ALL SUBSCRIBERS

LisaStrattin.com/Subscribe-Here

BOX SET

- FACTS ABOUT THE POISON DART FROGS
- FACTS ABOUT THE THREE TOED SLOTH
  - FACTS ABOUT THE RED PANDA
  - FACTS ABOUT THE SEAHORSE
  - FACTS ABOUT THE PLATYPUS
  - FACTS ABOUT THE REINDEER
  - FACTS ABOUT THE PANTHER
- FACTS ABOUT THE SIBERIAN HUSKY

LisaStrattin.com/BookBundle

Facts for Kids Picture Books by Lisa Strattin

Little Blue Penguin, Vol 92

Chipmunk, Vol 5

Frilled Lizard, Vol 39

Blue and Gold Macaw, Vol 13

Poison Dart Frogs, Vol 50

Blue Tarantula, Vol 115

African Elephants, Vol 8

Amur Leopard, Vol 89

Sabre Tooth Tiger, Vol 167

Baboon, Vol 174

Sign Up for New Release Emails Here

LisaStrattin.com/subscribe-here

Contents

INTRODUCTION

The emu is the largest bird native to Australia and the second largest bird in the world. Only the ostrich is larger. The emu is most commonly found in wooded areas, but they are common all over Australia.

CHARACTERISTICS

There are large emu farms in Australia, where the emu is bred for meat, oil and leather. Emu oil is said to hold medicinal healing properties when rubbed onto painful joints and is commonly used across the world mainly for sports injuries but also to help people suffering from arthritis.

They are nomadic animals which means that they rarely stay in the same place for long. This roaming lifestyle means that the emu can make the most of the food that is available where they are, and are known to travel long distances in order to find more food.

APPEARANCE

Emus have long necks and long legs in comparison to their body size. These long, flexible legs of the emu mean that the emu is able to run at high speeds, generally running at around 25 miles per hour!

Emus are able to reach a top speed of 30 miles per hour in short bursts (sprints) when the emu needs to get away quickly from a dangerous situation.

LIFE STAGES

Emus form breeding pairs during the Australian summer, which is in December, and mating usually occurs when the climate becomes colder a few months later. The female can lay up to 20 eggs (although 12 is the average number), which will hatch after a few months.

The male emu eats very little throughout the breeding process and it is he that incubates the eggs. By the time the emu chicks hatch, the male emu has lost a considerable amount of body weight and lives off of his fat reserves.

LIFE SPAN

Emus tend to live for between 10 and 20 years in the wild, although it is not uncommon for an emu to be more than 30 years old, especially when in captivity.

They are known to be very versatile animals and can easily adapt to many different environments.

SIZE

Emus can grow to over 6 feet tall and have very soft feathers. They are flightless birds mainly because of their enormous size, meaning that they are just too heavy to fly.

HABITAT

Studies show that emus seem to avoid dense forests and largely populated areas, so that they can be more aware of their surroundings. Although the emu prefers to be in woodland or shrubland where there is plenty to eat as well as cover to hide, they like to have a clear view of what is around them.

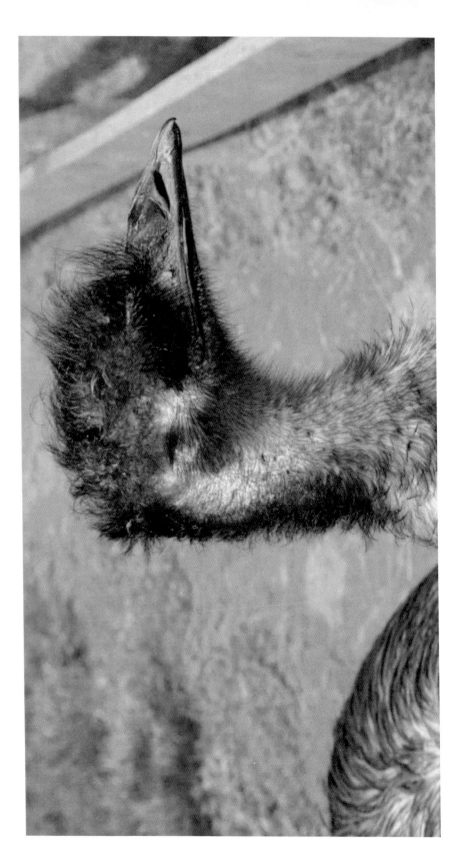

DIET

Emus are omnivorous birds feeding mostly on fruits, seeds and insects. They are generally found close to water and don't really like the more arid regions. However, the introduction of better water supplies to inland Australia has meant that although the populations have decreased of the wild emu, their home habitat range has expanded.

ENEMIES

Emus have few predators due to their large size and fast speed. They are most commonly preyed upon by wild dogs and crocodiles, and are hunted by humans. Emu eggs are eaten by many animals including dogs, birds of prey and large reptiles.

SUITABILITY AS PETS

They are a large, wild bird and not truly suitable to be a pet. Although they live alongside humans in Australia, they are not commonly considered a pet. You might check your local zoo to see if there are some kept in a habitat there, if you want to watch them.

COLOR ME

COLOR ME

COLOR ME

COLOR ME

COLOR ME

COLOR ME

COLOR ME

COLOR ME

COLOR ME

Please leave me a review here:

LisaStrattin.com/Review-Vol-245

For more Kindle Downloads Visit Lisa Strattin Author Page on Amazon Author Central

amazon.com/author/lisastrattin

To see upcoming titles, visit my website at LisaStrattin.com– most books available on Kindle!

LisaStrattin.com

FREE BOOK

FOR ALL SUBSCRIBERS – SIGN UP NOW

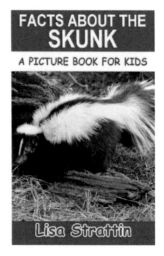

LisaStrattin.com/Subscribe-Here

LisaStrattin.com/Facebook

LisaStrattin.com/Youtube

Made in the USA
Coppell, TX
21 October 2023